Food and Festivals

A Flavour of MEXICO

Linda Illsley

WAYLAND

Cover photograph: A Mayan woman making *tortillas*.

Title page: People taking part in the Corpus Christi Festival in the city of Veracruz.

Contents page: A girl holding chillies.

All Wayland books encourage children to read and help them improve their literacy.

✓ The contents page, page numbers, headings and index help locate specific pieces of information.

✓ The glossary reinforces alphabetic knowledge and extends vocabulary.

✓ The further information section suggests other books dealing with the same subject.

✓ Find out more about how this book is specifically relevant to the National Literacy Strategy on page 31.

First published in 1998 by Wayland Publishers Limited, 61 Western Road, Hove, East Sussex, BN3 1JD, England

© Copyright 1998 Wayland Publishers Limited

Series editor: Polly Goodman
Book editor: Polly Goodman/Cath Senker
Assistant editor: Kate Davenport
Designer: Mark Whitchurch
Picture researcher: Paula Chapman

British Library Cataloguing in Publication Data
Illsley, Linda
    A Flavour of Mexico. – (Food and festivals)
    1. Cookery – Mexican – Juvenile literature
    2. Festivals – Mexico – Juvenile literature
    3. Food habits – Mexico – Juvenile literature
    4. Mexico - Social life and customs – Juvenile literature
    I. Title
    641.5'972

ISBN 0 7502 2222 0

Printed and bound in Italy by EuroGrafica, Vicenza.

Find Wayland on the Internet at http://www.wayland.co.uk

CONTENTS

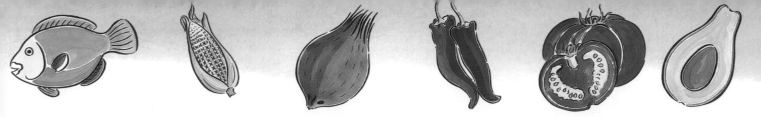

Mexico and its Food

USA

NEW MEXICO

MEXICO

Mexico's place in the world

MEXICO

GULF OF MEXICO

PACIFIC OCEAN

Guadalajara

JALISCO

Pátzcuaro

Uruapan

MICHOACAN

Mexico City

Veracruz

Puebla

Taxco

GUERRERO

Oaxaca

YUCATÁN

BELIZE

CHIAPAS

GUATEMALA

HONDURAS

EL SALVADOR

0   400 km

0   200 miles

Maize

Maize (sweetcorn) is a cereal which grows all over Mexico. It is the most important crop in the country.

Wheat

Wheat is also a cereal. It is used to make bread and cakes. Much wheat is grown in northern Mexico, where there is a good system of irrigation.

Chillies

Chillies have always been grown in Mexico. Most of the world's chillies still come from Mexico today.

Beans

Beans are another important Mexican food. They contain lots of protein. Beans come in many different colours and sizes.

Fish

There are many types of fish available in Mexico. Red snapper is very popular.

Meat

Beef and pork are the most popular meats in Mexico. Cattle ranches are mostly in the north of the country.

Food and Farming

Mexico is a country in North America, just below the USA. It covers an area of almost 2 million square kilometres. Most of Mexico is covered by mountains, which makes it difficult to grow food. The climate varies from the hot and dry north, to the humid heat of the south. The climate and landscape affect the types of food that are grown and the dishes that are prepared in each region.

There are many festivals in Mexico and food plays a very important part in them. Mexican food is usually made from fresh ingredients.

A farmer and his child on their small farm in Chiapas state.

Maize

Maize, which is also known as sweetcorn, has been grown all over Mexico for hundreds of years. It is often planted in the traditional way, with courgettes and beans growing alongside. Maize is used to prepare hundreds of Mexican dishes, such as *tortillas*, which most Mexicans eat every day. Special dishes, such as *tamales*, are made using ground maize.

▲ This painting shows the Tlaxcala Indians carrying and cooking maize in the early 1500s, about 500 years ago.

▼ A woman making *tortillas* in the traditional way.

GIFT FROM THE GODS

The Amerindians, who first lived in Mexico, believed that maize was a gift from the gods. It was a sacred food, used in religious festivals. When Spanish explorers arrived in Mexico in 1492, the Amerindians replaced maize with wheat as their sacred food.

Wheat

Wheat is grown all over Mexico, but it mostly grows in the north. Large irrigation systems have been built there to provide the crops with water. Wheat is used to make bread and cakes.

Festival bread

A special, traditional type of bread is made for the festival of the *Rosca de Reyes* (Day of the Three Wise Men), on 6 January each year. The bread has a tiny doll baked inside it. The person who gets the slice of bread containing the doll has to cook a meal for everyone else at a later date.

This bread has been ▶ specially prepared for the Day of the Dead (see page 22).

8

Chillies

More than 150 different types of chilli grow all over Mexico. They vary from the hottest chilli, called *habanero*, to the mild chilli, *güero*. Some chillies only grow in certain areas, such as the *chilhuacle*, which grows in Oaxaca. Chillies are used in lots of Mexican dishes. They add flavour and colour.

▼ These girls are holding a type of chilli that is used in New Mexico, USA.

FRESH OR DRIED CHILLIES

Chillies are used in many festival dishes. *Chiles en nogada* is a dish made with fresh chillies, called *anchos*, with meat, nuts, sultanas and *crème fraiche*.

Dried chillies are called *pasilla*. They are used to make other foods, such as *enchiladas*. *Enchiladas* are *tortillas* covered in chilli sauce, fried and served with cream and cheese.

▲ This stall shows the many different types of beans grown in Mexico.

Beans

Beans are the green pods of the bean plant, or the seeds inside the pods. Beans are very popular in Mexico as they grow easily, and are often planted next to maize crops. Beans are used in many Mexican recipes and lots of special dishes are prepared with them.

TRADITIONAL RELIGIONS

There are 56 different peoples living in Mexico. Many follow the Roman Catholic religion, but they also keep some of their traditional religions and customs. For example, in some towns, live turkeys decorated with flower necklaces are carried to church as an offering. This tradition is believed to come from a pre-Columbian custom of sacrificing animals as offerings to the gods.

▲ At this festival in Oaxaca, a man carries a turkey decorated with flowers.

Meat

Meat is a favourite type of food in Mexico, so it is always served on special occasions and at festivals. In the north, there is a lot of grazing land, so beef is more common. In the mountains and rain forests of the centre and the south, it is easier to raise smaller animals, such as goats, pigs, chickens and turkeys.

These chickens are ▶ being sold at a market.

Family Celebrations

About 90 per cent of Mexicans are Roman Catholics. The Catholic religion was brought to Mexico by the Spanish in 1492.

Baptisms

Many Mexicans are baptized in church. There is a special baptism Mass (church service), to which all friends and relatives are invited. As they leave the church, the godparents of the baptized baby often throw coins into the air for the guests to catch. Children have fun running to try and catch the coins!

◀ These young girls are standing outside a church in Jalisco.

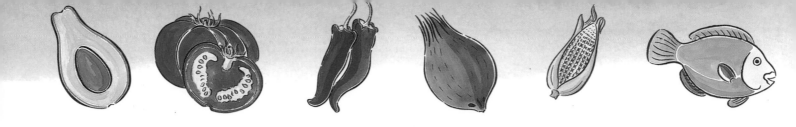

Party!

After the baptism Mass, there is a party in a hired hall, or in the home of the baby's parents. A variety of food is served.

If the Mass is held in the morning, then a dish called *tamales* is often served. *Tamale* is a light, maize-flavoured dough, which is wrapped in maize leaves and steamed. If the Mass takes place in the afternoon, people often eat a dish called *mole*. *Mole* has twenty-eight ingredients, which include nuts, raisins, aniseed, chocolate and three types of chilli. It is a kind of sauce that is served with turkey or chicken, and rice.

▼ *Tamales* served with a bowl of *mole*.

Birthdays

Many babies are named after Catholic saints. As they grow up, they celebrate the saint's birthday, as well as their own birthday. This means that Mexicans have two birthday parties a year!

A decorated cake and ice-cream are often served at birthday parties, but dishes such as *pozole* and *tostadas* are also birthday favourites. *Pozole* is a soup or stew with meat, maize kernels (grains) and chillies. It is served with lemon, onion, oregano and cabbage. *Tostadas* are fried maize *tortillas* topped with chicken and beans, or pork and avocado. Cabbage, cream, cheese and *salsa* are eaten with *tostadas*.

▼ This is a typical 'Sweet Fifteen' birthday party, traditionally a big day for girls in Mexico.

Party game

A favourite game at Mexican children's parties is the traditional game of *piñata*. To make a *piñata*, a clay pot is filled with sweets and fruit. It is covered with newspaper and decorated with colourful strips of paper to look like a figure or an animal. The *piñata* is hung up high.

Children queue for their turn to be blindfolded and given a stick, which they use to try and break the swinging *piñata*. When it is finally broken, everybody tries to grab the goodies that are inside!

▲ This fruit stall in Mexico City has different types of *piñatas* hanging above it.

Weddings

▼ There is a recipe for making these Mexican wedding biscuits on the opposite page.

Weddings can be the biggest event in many Mexicans' lives. More than 200 people are often invited to the church ceremony and to the party afterwards.

At the party, after the wedding meal, the newly-weds cut a wedding cake covered with white icing sugar. There is usually a band for the guests to dance to, and the party may go on all night!

▼ *Mariachi* bands are very popular at Mexican weddings.

16

Wedding Biscuits

INGREDIENTS

100 g Pecan nuts

250 g Unsalted butter, left out to soften

100 g Icing sugar

375 g White self-raising flour

EQUIPMENT

Greased baking tray
Chopping knife
Chopping board
Food processor

Large bowl
Wooden spoon
Sugar sifter

1 Heat the oven to 180° C. Roughly chop half the pecan nuts. Put the other half in the food processor and grind them.

2 Put the butter, flour and half the sugar into the bowl. Mix together to form a dough.

3 Add the pecan nuts and mix. Shape into small balls (about 3 cm across) and place them on the baking tray. Put the tray in the middle of the oven.

4 Bake for 10–15 minutes. Ask an adult to take the tray out of the oven. When the biscuits are cool, sift sugar on to them.

Always be careful with hot ovens. Ask an adult to help you.

Easter

There are many religious festivals in Mexico throughout the year. Easter is probably one of the most important Christian festivals. On Good Friday, people remember Christ dying on the cross, and on Easter Sunday, they celebrate him coming back to life. During Lent (the forty days before Easter Sunday), Catholics eat fish or lentils instead of meat. This helps them to remember the time that Jesus spent in the desert without food.

▼ Amerindian people acting out the events of Easter in a play.

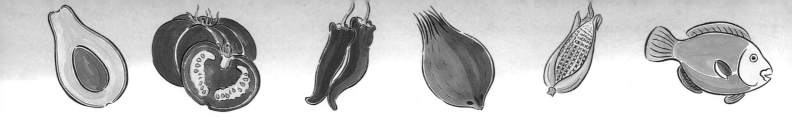

Easter processions

Some towns, such as Taxco and Iztapalapa (part of Mexico City), are famous for their Easter processions. The processions are always accompanied by bands of musicians.

People come from far away, either to watch or to take part in the processions. There are often many street stalls selling many different types of food and drinks to the visitors.

This is a religious ▶ procession in Yucatán.

19

Easter pottery

In some cities, such as Uruapan, there are special markets selling colourful, handmade pottery. It is traditional to buy a pot and give it to a friend. On the Saturday before Easter Sunday, you have to be careful if you walk through the streets, since it is also traditional to throw buckets of water over passers-by!

▲ This is Mexican lentil soup with parsley, served with a *tortilla*. Follow the recipe opposite to make it yourself.

These women in Puebla are ▶ buying pots to give to their friends as traditional Easter gifts.

Lentil Soup

INGREDIENTS

2 Tablespoons oil
1/2 Onion, finely chopped
1 Clove garlic, chopped
4 Bacon rashers, cut into thin strips
3 Tomatoes, chopped

185 g Lentils, washed
1 Bay leaf
2 Carrots, diced
1 Litre water
Parsley
Salt and pepper, to taste

EQUIPMENT

Large saucepan
Wooden spoon

1 Put the oil, onion, garlic and bacon in the saucepan and cook on a medium heat until the onion changes colour.

2 Add the tomatoes and cook for a few minutes, stirring constantly. Add the other ingredients, except the parsley.

3 Bring the mixture to the boil over a high heat. Turn the heat down and simmer until the lentils are soft, stirring regularly.

4 Ask an adult to taste the soup. Add a little salt and pepper. Serve in soup bowls with some parsley in the middle. Eat with bread or *tortillas.*

Always be careful with hot liquids. Ask an adult to help you.

The Day of the Dead

The Day of the Dead is a Mexican festival, which is based on a mixture of Catholic and Amerindian beliefs. Preparations for this festival take a lot of time. Special flowers are planted months ahead, and bread-baking ovens are built a week or so beforehand.

▼ A girl in Michoacan decorating a grave for the Day of the Dead.

Cleaning the graves

On the last day of October, everyone who has a dead friend or relative goes to the cemetery and cleans the person's grave. Then people decorate the grave with candles and flowers. At home, they build an altar and place a photograph of the dead person in the centre.

▲ This is an altar in a family home in Guerrero. There is a photo of the dead relatives.

◄ On the Day of the Dead, it is traditional to spend the day at the graves of relatives.

23

Food offerings

Various types of food are placed on the altar or grave as an offering to the dead person. Many Mexicans believe that the soul of a dead person returns on the Day of the Dead, shares a meal, spends some time with friends and relatives, and then returns to the world of the dead. Mexicans show their respect for death on this day.

◀ This is a decorated sugar skull for the Day of the Dead.

SUGAR SKULLS

On the Day of the Dead, it is traditional to buy sugar skulls to decorate the altar and the home. Sugar skulls are sold on special stalls in markets. The foreheads of the skulls have a space where a name is written in sugar icing. People often buy a skull for the dead person, as well as one skull for each living family member.

◀ *Salsa* is a common dish made for the Day of the Dead. Follow the recipe opposite to make some.

Salsa

EQUIPMENT

Chopping board   Bowl
Knife   Spoon

INGREDIENTS

1 Small onion or
   6 spring onions
2 Large, ripe tomatoes
Juice of 1 lime
Salt to taste
A few coriander leaves

Chop the onion or spring onions into small pieces.

Put the onion into the bowl. Add the lime juice and a pinch of salt.

Wash the tomatoes and the coriander and chop them into small pieces. Add them to the bowl and mix everything together with a spoon.

Leave the mixture for five minutes and then taste it to see if it needs more salt. Serve with *tacos* (filled *tortillas*), grilled meat or *tortilla* chips.

Always be careful when using knives. Ask an adult to help you.

Christmas

Christmas is a Christian festival celebrating the birth of Christ. Christmas celebrations start early in Mexico, with traditional *posadas*, or nativity plays. These take place every night for the fourteen days before Christmas Day. Mexicans gather together with neighbours and friends to act out the story of Joseph and Mary's journey to Bethlehem. At the end of the play, parcels of sweets and fruit are given out.

▼ This is Guadalajara Cathedral, with a special nativity scene outside it for Christmas.

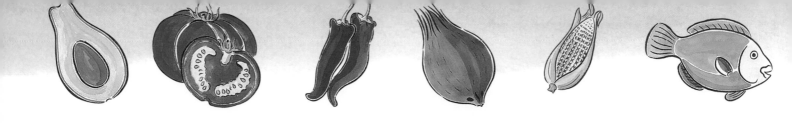

▲ Christmas decorations on sale at a fair in Pátzcuaro.

Christmas Eve

Mexicans have Christmas dinner on Christmas Eve in the evening. The morning of Christmas Eve is very busy, because all the dishes for the big evening meal must be prepared. Stuffed turkey, *mole, tamales, buñuelos* (doughnuts), salads, cakes and other sweets are all traditional Christmas food.

There is a special Christmas Mass at church, where family and friends gather before the evening meal.

27

Dinner and dancing

▼ This is a delicious Mexican Christmas drink. There is a recipe for it on the opposite page.

After Mass, many families go home to break a *piñata*. Some have two *piñatas* – one for the children, and a second one for the adults.

At the stroke of midnight, everyone hugs each other and wishes one another a merry Christmas. They open presents while dinner is served. After dinner, music is played for everyone to dance to, often until the next morning!

Christmas Drink

EQUIPMENT

Large saucepan
Bowl
Strainer

INGREDIENTS

150 g Tamarinds, peeled
1/2 Litre water
100 g Sultanas
15 Pitted prunes
5 Cloves

10 Fresh guavas, cut into small pieces (or 2 cans, drained and chopped)
1 Cinammon stick
Sugar to taste

Put the tamarinds and water into the saucepan. Bring to the boil and allow to simmer for 20 minutes.

Add more water, the cinammon stick and cloves and half the fruit. Simmer for at least one hour.

Add some sugar. Ask an adult to taste the drink – it should be sweet, but not too sweet. Simmer for another 5 minutes, until the sugar has dissolved.

Strain the liquid into a bowl. Allow the drink to cool slightly. Then pour into heat-proof glasses and decorate with the other half of the fruit.

Be careful with the hot pan. Ask an adult to help you pour the drink.

Glossary

Amerindians The native people of Mexico.

Baptism The Christian ceremony in which a person, often a baby, is welcomed into the Church.

Cereal Any grass that produces a grain which can be eaten, such as wheat, maize or rice.

Godparent A family friend who agrees at a child's baptism to help him or her to learn about the Christian religion.

Grazing land Land where animals, such as cows, feed on grass.

Irrigation Bringing water to dry areas to help food crops to grow better.

***Mariachi* bands** Bands of strolling musicians who sing and play guitars, violins and trumpets.

Mass A Roman Catholic service with a ceremony that celebrates Christ's death and coming to life again.

Pre-Columbian The time before 1492, when Christopher Columbus arrived in the Americas.

Ranch A large area of land used for raising farm animals, usually cattle.

Roman Catholic A Christian religion headed by the Pope.

Sacred Having special religious meaning.

Soul The spirit of a person, which is believed to live on after the person has died.

Tortilla A thin pancake made from ground maize and cooked on a hot, flat pan until it is dry.

Photograph and artwork acknowledgements
The publishers would like to thank the following for allowing their pictures to be used in this book:
Andes (Carlos Reyes-Manzo) 14; Chapel Studios (Zul Mukhida) 16 (top), 20 (top), 28; Getty Images (David Hiser) 20 (bottom); Hutchison (Liba Taylor) 8; Linda Illsley 10, 19; Image Bank (Guido Rossi) 5 (bottom left), (Jurgen Vogt) 12; James Davis Travel Photography (Eye Ubiquitous) 16 (bottom); Magnum *Cover photo*; Mexicolore (Sean Sprague) 18; Panos (Ron Giling) 6, (Liba Taylor) 13; South American Pictures (C. Lipson) 9, 11 (bottom), (Tony Morrison) 15, (Tony Morrison) 27; Trip (Ask Images) *Title page*, (C. Caffrey) 11 (top), (E. James) 22, (A. Deutsch) 23 (bottom), (C. Caffrey) 26; Mireuille Vautier 5 (top left), 5 (bottom right), 7 (top), 23 (top), 24 (top); Wayland Picture Library (Chapel Studios) 24 (bottom).

Fruit and vegetable artwork is by Tina Barber. The map artwork on page 4 is by Hardlines. The step-by-step recipe artwork is by Judy Stevens.

Topic Web and Resources

MATHS
Using and understanding data and measures (recipes).

Using and reading measuring instruments: scales.

Using weights and measures.

Using and understanding fractions.

SCIENCE
Food and nutrition.

Health.

Plants in different habitats.

Plants as a life process.

Mixing and dissolving different materials.

Changing materials through heat.

GEOGRAPHY
Locality study.

Landscapes and climate.

Farming.

Influence of landscape on human activities: farming and food festivals.

Awareness of wider context of a place.

DESIGN AND TECHNOLOGY
Design a poster to advertise a food product.

Technology used in food production.

Food preparation.

Follow a recipe.

Food & Festivals TOPIC WEB

HISTORY
Trace the history of modern British food.

Investigate the different farming methods used over the past century.

MODERN FOREIGN LANGUAGES
Language skills.

Everyday activities: food.

People, places and customs.

MUSIC
As part of celebration.

Music from a different culture.

Musical instruments.

ENGLISH
Make up a slogan to sell a food product.

Write a poem or story using food as the subject.

Write a menu for a Mexican meal.

R.E.
Food and Festivals.

Christianity:

Easter; Christmas; Baptism; Death.

OTHER BOOKS TO READ

A Feast of Festivals by Hugo Slim (Pickering, 1996)

Celebrate Christian Festivals by Jan Thompson (Heinemann, 1997)

Country Fact Files: Mexico by Edward Parker (Macdonald Young Books, 1995)

Country Insights: Mexico by Edward Parker (Wayland, 1997)

Festivals: Christmas by Kerena Marchant (Wayland, 1996)

Festivals: Easter by Philip Sauvain (Wayland, 1997)

Fiesta!: Mexico (Watts, 1997)

This book meets the following specific objectives of the National Literacy Strategy's Framework for Teaching:

✔ Range of work in non-fiction: simple recipes (especially Year 2, Term 1), instructions, labels, captions, lists, glossary, index.

✔ Vocabulary extension: words linked to particular topics (food words) and technical words from work in other subjects (geography and food science).

Index

Page numbers in **bold** mean there is a photograph on the page.